Library of Congress Catalog Card Number: 64-19694
Printed in the United States of America

2   3   4   5

LET'S FIND OUT ABOUT
OUR FLAG

by
MARTHA AND CHARLES SHAPP
Pictures by Henry S. Gillette

FRANKLIN WATTS, INC.
575 Lexington Avenue, New York 22

Did you know that our flag has a birthday?
Every year on June 14, we celebrate the flag's birthday.
We call that day Flag Day.

Long, long ago there was no American flag.
Our country belonged to England and the English
flag was flown in this country.

About two hundred years ago Americans decided that they
    wanted to be free.
They decided to fight for their freedom and went to war
    against England.

The Americans needed their own flag.
George Washington and other leaders of our country looked
over many different designs for flags.
On June 14, 1777, they chose one to be the new American flag.

George Washington showed
    the design to Betsy Ross
    and asked her to
    make the new flag.

That first American flag had 13 stripes and 13 stars because at that time there were only 13 colonies.

Today our flag still has 13 stripes, but now it has 50 stars.
The stripes stand for the original 13 colonies.
Each star stands for one state of the United States.

Our flag has many names. You will hear it called "Old Glory." Sometimes it is called "The Red, White and Blue," and sometimes, "The Stars and Stripes."

The national anthem of our country is a song about our flag.
The song is called "The Star-Spangled Banner."
This song has a story.

In 1812 our country had another war with England. The English had captured an American and kept him a prisoner on an English ship.

Another American named Francis Scott Key went to the English ship to ask that his friend be set free.

The English agreed to let Francis Scott Key
and his friend go.
But just then English warships began to bomb an American
fort.
Francis Scott Key and his friend were not able to leave the
ship.

22

All night long the bombing went on.
The two Americans kept watching the fort.
Would the fort have to surrender?

24

They knew that so long as the flag flew the fort was safe.
Francis Scott Key kept looking for the flag.

At last the night was over.
In the dawn's early light, Francis Scott Key saw the flag
 still flying!

The fort had not surrendered!

Happily, Francis Scott Key began to write.
He wrote the song we all sing to our flag.

"O say can you see, by the dawn's early light,
What so proudly we hail'd at the twilight's
last gleaming,
Whose broad stripes and bright stars through
the perilous fight
O'er the ramparts we watch'd, were so gallantly
streaming?
And the rocket's red glare, the bomb bursting
in air,
Gave proof through the night that our flag
was still there,
O say does that star-spangled banner yet wave
O'er the land of the free and the home of the
brave?"

33

Americans honor their flag and they follow certain rules
when they fly the flag.
You must never let the flag touch the ground.
Never leave the flag out on a rainy or stormy day.

The flag is flown only in the daytime.
It is taken down every night.

Our flag flies over all public buildings.
There is a flag flying over your school.
When an important person dies, the flag hangs at half-mast.

On Flag Day, on the Fourth of July, and on other holidays many people hang flags from their windows.

On many holidays there are parades.
Men and boys always take their hats off when the flag
passes by.

In school we pledge allegiance to our flag.
"I pledge allegiance to the flag of the United States of
America and to the Republic for which it stands;
one nation under God, indivisible, with liberty and justice
for all."

To people all over the world,

our flag is the Flag of Liberty.

VOCABULARY LIST

a
able
about
against
ago
agreed
air
all
allegiance
always
America
American (s)
an
and
another
anthem
are
as
ask (ed)
at

banner
be
because
began
belonged
birthday
blue
bomb (ing)
boys
brave
bright
broad
buildings
bursting
but
by

call (ed)
can
captured
celebrate

certain
chose
colonies
country

day
daytime
dawn's
decided
design (s)
did
dies
different
does
down

each
early
England
English
every

fight
first
flag (s)
flew
flies
flown
fly (ing)
follow
for
fort
fourth
free
freedom
friend
from

gallantly
gave
glare

gleaming
glory
go
God
ground

had
hail'd
half-mast
hang (s)
happily
has
hats
have
he
hear
her
him
his
holidays
home
honor
hundred

I
important
in
indivisible
is
it

July
June
just
justice

kept
knew
know

land
last

leaders
leave
let
liberty
light
long
looked
looking

make
many
men
must

named
names
nation
national
needed
never
new
night
no
not
now

o
o'er
of
off
old
on
one
only
or
original
other
our
out
over
own

parades
passes

people
perilous
person
pledge
prisoner
proof
proudly
public

rainy
ramparts
red
republic
rocket's
rules

safe
saw
say
school
see
set
ship
showed
sing
sometimes
so
song
spangled
stand (s)
star (s)
state (s)
still
stormy
story
streaming
stripes
surrender (ed)

take
taken
that
the

their
there
then
they
time
this
through
to
today
touch
twilight's
two

under
united

wanted
war
warships
was
watch'd
watching
wave
we
went
were
what
when
which
white
whose
will
windows
with
world
would
write
wrote

year (s)
yet
you
your